Pirate Slang

for Modern Day Use

Pirate Slang
for Modern Day Use

Ricky Adams

Published by Pirate Slang Press

TikTok @pirateslang

ISBN: 9798330306039

Printed in the United States of America

1st Edition

Step aboard me matey, and learn some pirate slang. Were you aware that pirates in the early 1700s had a distinct slang all their own? Most of these words have vanished from the English language. It's about time we start including these back into our everyday conversations. Impress and amaze your friends, family, and colleagues with your new sea worthy talk. You can tap into the essence of a character from your favorite pirate movie or simply add some saltiness to your everyday chats. Developing fluency in pirate slang will elevate your authenticity and reveal your true inner pirate at heart.

Addle

-Gross water-

"Dude this water is straight up addle. Did you get it from the sewer? I'm not drinking this trash."

Ahoy

-Hello-

"Ahoy mom, I'm home from school."

Aye

-yes-

"Aye, I did watch that horrible movie, but I won't be watching it again."

Blimey!

-Surprised exclamation-

"Blimey! I was not expecting the line to be this long for a cronut. It's like 300 people deep!"

Blow Me Down!

-Shock-

"Well blow me down! I wasn't expecting that operation to hurt so much."

Blow The Gaff

-Revealing a secret-

"Welp I really blew the gaff on that one. I thought Karen already knew her haircut was sus."

Booty

-Treasure-

"I found the real booty, it's the candy aisle at the gas station. Pure gold my friend."

Bring a Spring Upon 'Er'

-Turn a different direction-

"I thought the burger place was this way, but I think we need to bring a spring upon er' and try going down this street instead."

Bring your Arse to Anchor

-Sit down-

"Tommy it's time to bring your arse to the anchor and eat dinner. No more messing around."

Chivey

-Knife-

"This steak is as tough as concrete. I need a chivey to cut this up."

Crackle Fruit

-Eggs-

"I'm telling you my mom makes the best crackle fruit. Hands down better than your mom."

Double Dutch

-Nonsense-

"Did you get hit in the head or something?
Your talking pure double Dutch."

Duds

-Bad clothes-

"I need to go to the mall, seriously, all I have is duds in my closet. Time to step up this wardrobe"

Foul Up

-Make a mistake-

"Man, my review at work was rough this year. They had a whole list of projects I fouled up."

Go on account

-Turning into a pirate-

"After finding this pirate slang book I think it's time I go fully on account and order my jacket, hat, and sword offline."

Hands

-Ship's crew-

"Bro, don't even start something. You know me and my hands mean business."

Hang the Jib

-Frown-

"Listen I know you really liked her Kev, but it's time to stop hanging the jib and get back out on that dance floor."

Hearties

-Friends-

"My hearties and I had a blast at the waterpark yesterday...that is until the code brown happened in the lazy river."

Hornswoggle

-Tricked-

"Welp I straight up got Hornswoggled. This is not a real 1st edition holo gem collectable card. It's just some knock off."

Landlubber

-Clumsy person-

"I never go to that coffee shop. A bunch of landlubbers run it, and five times out of ten they get my order wrong. who would want a 5 shot espresso latte? I couldn't sleep for days."

Loot

-Stolen goods-

"I left my loot in my locker and somebody straight up swiped it. I'm so bummed."

Marooned

-Abandoned-

"My friends and I were supposed to all meet at the park at 11am sharp, but no one showed. It seems as if they have marooned me at this playground."

Mate

-Friend-

"This is my mate Jim. He can turn his eyelids inside out...want to see?"

Mutiny

-Revolt-

"Jim has gone too far with these lunch time meetings. I think it's time we stood up to him. It'd be right time for a mutiny of the office."

Pistol Proof

-Lucky-

"My blackjack game is just pistol proof.
Dealer can't touch my 21 game."

Pull Your Finger Out

-Stop hesitating-

"Dude it's time to pull your finger out and just go ask Karen on a date."

Ramshackle

-Discombobulated-

"Your room is literally a ramshackle. I can barley step a foot inside, and how old is that bag of food? It smells like a dumpster fire in here."

Sea Legs

-Used to standing on a boat-

"I know you've only been working here a couple of weeks, but it really does seem like you have your sea legs now. Do you want to try the closing shift this week?"

Show a Leg

-Wake up quick-

"Show a leg Karen! The waterpark opens in thirty minutes and your still in bed."

Sloppes

-Baggy clothes-

"I love how the sloppes jeans of the 90's are coming back in style. They're so comfy!"

Talk Bilge

-Nonsense-

"That guy at the bar was talking bilge left and right. He said he works in finance, but the advice he was giving was horrible."